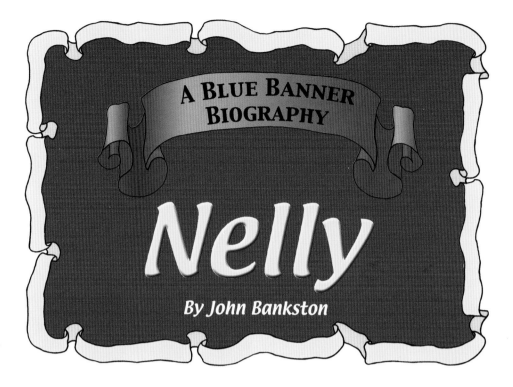

A BLUE BANNER BIOGRAPHY

Nelly

By John Bankston

Mitchell Lane
PUBLISHERS

P.O. Box 196
Hockessin, DE 19707
Visit us on the web: www.mitchelllane.com
Comments? email us: mitchelllane@mitchelllane.com

Mitchell Lane
PUBLISHERS

Printing   4   5   6   7   8   9

Blue Banner Biographies

Alicia Keys	Allen Iverson	Ashanti
Ashlee Simpson	Ashton Kutcher	Avril Lavigne
Beyoncé	Bow Wow	Britney Spears
Christina Aguilera	Christopher Paul Curtis	Clay Aiken
Condoleezza Rice	Daniel Radcliffe	Derek Jeter
Eminem	Eve	Ja Rule
Jay-Z	Jennifer Lopez	J.K. Rowling
Jodie Foster	Justin Berfield	Kate Hudson
Lance Armstrong	Lindsay Lohan	Mario
Mary-Kate and Ashley Olsen	Melissa Gilbert	Michael Jackson
Missy Elliott	**Nelly**	P. Diddy
Paris Hilton	Queen Latifah	Ritchie Valens
Rita Williams-Garcia	Ron Howard	Rudy Giuliani
Sally Field	Selena	Shirley Temple
Usher		

Library of Congress Cataloging-in-Publication Data
Bankston, John, 1974-
        Nelly / John Bankston.
            p. cm. — (A blue banner biography)
Includes bibliographical references (p.   ), discography, and index.
        ISBN 1-58415-218-4
        1. Nelly (Rapper)—Juvenile literature. 2. Rap musicians—United States—Biography—Juvenile literature. I. Title. II. Series.
        ML3930.N45B36 2003
        782.421649'092--dc21
                                                                                                2003004740

ABOUT THE AUTHOR: Born in Boston, Massachussetts, John Bankston began publishing articles in newspapers and magazines while still a teenager. Since then, he has written over two hundred articles, and contributed chapters to books such as *Crimes of Passion,* and *Death Row 2000,* which have been sold in bookstores across the world. He has written numerous biographies for young adults, including *Mandy Moore* and *Alexander Fleming and the Story of Penicillin* (Mitchell Lane). He currently lives in Portland, Oregon.

PHOTO CREDITS: Cover: Frederick M. Brown/Getty Images; p. 4 AP Photo/Michael Caulfield; p. 8 Matt Stroshane/Getty Images; p. 12 Ethan Miller/Corbis; p. 15 AP Photo/Reed Saxon; p. 20 Frank Micelotta/Getty Images; p. 22 Kevin Winter/Getty Images; p. 25 AP Photo/Joe Cavaretta; p. 26 Reuters NewMedia Inc./Corbis; p. 28 AP Photo/Lucy Nicholson

CONTENTS

Arriving at Los Angeles's Staples Center, rap artist Nelly had come a long way from St. Louis. When he first began rapping, Nelly was a baseball player looking for a way to help out his mom. His success means being able to help his family, and perform before a large audience like the one at the 2001 Grammy Awards.

Rough Streets

*C*ornell Haynes faced a difficult choice.

When he was 15, he and several friends in St. Louis, Missouri had formed a band known as the St. Lunatics. Everyone had a nickname, and Cornell's would eventually become famous: Nelly.

But that fame was still far away. Even though they had a single that became a local hit, the five years since their start had been a struggle. In spite of the difficulties, the band was determined to stay together.

"We're all family," Nelly explained to *Teen People*. "We came up together from nothing."

Then they finally got a break. A national record company was interested. But that interest came with one condition. The company didn't want the St. Lunatics. They only wanted Nelly. Now it looked like Nelly was going to have to go out on his own. A record deal was going to split them apart.

Nelly was used to being on his own. But he wasn't going to forget the ones who helped him make it.

Cornell Haynes Jr. was born on November 2, 1978 to Rhoda Mack and Cornell Haynes Sr. in Austin, Texas. Cornell Sr. was a sergeant in the U.S. Air Force and for the first few years of Nelly's life the Haynes family moved frequently. For a time they even lived on a military base in Spain.

Nelly was used to being on his own. But he wasn't going to forget the ones who helped him make it.

The family eventually settled in St. Louis, Missouri. Perhaps one of the most racially divided cities in the United States, it rests along the eastern edge of the state of Missouri where the Mississippi and Missouri Rivers come together.

Although Missouri sits squarely in the Midwest, Nelly has said in interviews that he considers it a part of the South because it was a "former slave state." During the years leading up to the Civil War, Missouri allowed its residents to own slaves even as neighboring free states outlawed the practice.

In 1860, over 100,000 of the state's residents were slaves. They represented nearly 10 percent of the population. The slave owners mainly lived along the edges of the Mississippi River, the main route to the southern businesses that bought the crops the slaves helped to harvest. The urban areas had few slaves and most of their residents opposed the practice. This stress between urban and rural, slave owners and abolitionists (people who were against slavery) mirrored the one on the national level which led to the Civil War.

Although Missouri remained in the Union, many of the state's leaders supported the southern states that seceded to form the Confederate States of America. After the war, thousands of African Americans migrated north from plantations in Mississippi, Louisiana and Alabama, settling in growing St. Louis. While the city is best known for its towering Gateway Arch, it also has a reputation for crime and grit. For Nelly, it was the place where he grew up, often unsupervised. As he explained on his web site www.nelly.net, "It's so small that everybody knows each other. I've got a love-hate relationship with it."

> *St. Louis has an unmistakable southern flavor, which in some ways gives the whole area a small town feel.*

The city has an unmistakable southern flavor from the food to the accents, which in some ways gives the whole area a small town feel, similar to other urban

From hip-hop's fringes to pop music superstardom, Nelly has embraced every aspect of his rise to success. Here he joins NSYNC's Justin Timberlake at the Challenge for the Children IV event.

areas in the south like Charleston, South Carolina and Savannah, Georgia.

Yet as difficult as St. Louis could be for young Nelly, it wasn't as hard as his home life. Even as a little kid, Nelly realized his parents were having problems. When he was eight years old, they divorced, a decision which had an immediate impact on his life. Without a father around, he began hanging with older boys. Sometimes they helped him and gave him advice. Sometimes they got him in trouble.

"There was a time when my mother couldn't afford to keep me," he admitted to *Rolling Stone*, "and my father couldn't afford to keep me, so I lived with friends, grandparents. When you're a kid, that affects you. You don't see that it's not because they don't want you. That's why you rebel."

In the beginning, Nelly's rebellion meant taking out his rage on other kids. He got into a lot of fights, and sometimes the fights got him kicked out of school. Other times his mother would pull him out, hoping his behavior would change. It didn't. By the time he reached junior high, he had attended at least eight different schools.

> *After his parents' divorce, Nelly got into a lot of fights, and sometimes the fights got him kicked out of school.*

"I had chips in my shoulder," he told Steven Chean in an article in *USA Weekend*. "The only way I got over that is, my mama always said she was coming back for me, and she did." She became his role model, working at fast-food restaurants to support him.

Then she made a decision.

She decided to leave St. Louis for the nearby suburb of University City. She hoped the quieter, safer streets of University City would be better for her son. The move helped turn Nelly's attention from fights to sports. It also gave him a chance to demonstrate his new-found talent for rapping. Unfortunately, in University City he also discovered a way to make money that might have taken all of his dreams away.

> *Moving to University City gave Nelly a chance to demonstrate his new-found talent for rapping.*

Field of Broken Dreams

*I*n University City, Nelly focused on playing baseball. He quickly became a star.

Before he'd gotten picked on because of his size. Now his compact frame was perfect for playing shortstop. Instead of fighting he was succeeding. By the time he reached University High School, college scouts and even a few professional teams were noticing his talent. Baseball did more than get him noticed. It also taught him how to handle stress.

"I never felt pressure, just the energy and excitement of 'Let's get it rolling,'" he told *Teen People*.

The sport also introduced him to several people who would influence his life. One of them was Robert Cleveland, a fellow hip-hop fan who went by the stage name of Kyjuan. Nelly's fellow baseball player quickly noticed his teammate's rap talents.

Even when he was part of a group, Nelly stood out. As the St. Lunatics gained notice, Nelly was singled out for solo recognition. Here he performs at the Radio Music Awards on November 4, 2000.

When the two were 14, they sat down and wrote their first song. It was called "Addiction," and in many ways it predicted Nelly's future. Except he was never addicted to drugs. He was addicted to money.

Kyjuan and Nelly played baseball, and imagined a future where their single moms wouldn't have to work two or three jobs just to make ends meet. They dreamed of getting out of poverty. For a while it looked like that path might lie between the white chalk lines of a baseball diamond.

Nelly was still in high school when the St. Louis Amateur Baseball Association recruited him to play. Although amateur leagues are mainly a mishmash of the "almost weres" and "never wases," for a young player like Nelly it seemed to be a clear stepping stone to playing in the majors. Both the Atlanta Braves and the Pittsburgh Pirates were showing a lot of interest in him. "I really thought that I'd be playing ball," he explains on his web site.

It wasn't that easy. He was skilled but not skilled enough to reach the majors right away. Reaching a professional level as a baseball player could take years. "Baseball to me was a slow, grinding process, and I wanted the fast money and all that," he told *Sports Illustrated*. "So, I kind of got out of the baseball thing and went back to the hood."

"I was down in the hood, and the money was flowing," he explained to *Rolling Stone*. "A bat and a ball. That was taking too long. It was the wrong attitude to take."

> **Nelly was skilled in baseball, but not skilled enough to reach the majors right away.**

Nelly left high school. He left baseball. And he embraced an attitude that led him down a dangerous street, one familiar to many of today's top hip-hop artists. Nelly Haynes began dealing drugs.

Making a
Decision

By the time many of his classmates were ready to graduate from high school, Nelly was living on his own. He worked part-time at a fast-food restaurant and paid rent on a small apartment. Although he'd dropped out of high school, some of his peers thought he had it made.

To an outsider, Nelly seemed to have it all. He had cash in his pocket, nice clothes, a decent ride. There was only one problem. His paycheck didn't cover everything. Most of his money came from dealing drugs.

Nelly thought he needed the money. He was about to become a father. Although the mother has remained unidentified, in 1996 she gave birth to Cornell's daughter Chanel. Three years later they'd have a son Tre. Nelly always felt that his father had let him down by not supporting him. He was determined not to make the same mistake.

Nelly never intended to be a solo act. Instead he was part of the St. Lunatics. Here he appears with them at the American Music Awards. (Top, L to R: Kyjuan, Nelly, Ali, Murphy Lee; Bottom: Slo Down)

But long before he was old enough to vote, he saw what was happening to the older dealers—they were winding up in jail or shot. He was smart enough to see what his future would be if he kept dealing drugs. That is, there was no future at all.

Playing sports was out. If he stopped dealing, that left him with a single dream: music. In 1993, he'd pulled together his crew at University High—best friend Kyjuan (Robert Cleveland), Murphy Lee (Tohri Harper), Big Lee (Ali Jones) and his half-brother, City Spud (Lavell Webb)—and formed the St. Lunatics. Slo Down (Corey Edwards) was added in 1996.

Nelly was fortunate to realize early that he wouldn't have much of a future if he kept dealing drugs.

For Nelly, even then the dealing didn't stop. "There was a point in St. Louis where dope was your currency," he told *Rolling Stone*. "Whoever was bringing in the most work did the most, basically. As far as reputation, the more work you had the bigger you were in rap."

In other words, the more he dealt, the better his connections in St. Louis became and the greater his chances of performing at the top hip-hop clubs and getting his music played on the radio.

It was a dangerous situation. Fortunately it didn't last long.

A local production company liked what they heard and financed the St. Lunatics' CD. Nelly was just 18, and it looked like the opportunity of a lifetime. Although Nelly claims he and his crew saw little money from the deal, it put the group's name on the lips of many St. Louis fans.

In 1996, the album's first single, "Gimme What Ya Got," was played regularly at the top St. Louis hip-hop spot, Club Casino. A local radio station picked it up as well, and soon the song was being heard regularly between hits from the coasts. Fans began buying the CD and it went on to sell nearly 10,000 copies. For music produced and financed by an unknown, independent label, that is an extraordinary number. But even though his CD was selling so well, Nelly still couldn't get a meeting at the major record labels.

Nelly was willing to do whatever he had to do to put St. Louis and the St. Lunatics on the map.

He worried that it was the St. Louis factor. Hip-hop was a coastal industry. Its fans lived around the country, but most of the rappers and producers, along with the labels which supported them, were located in either California or New York.

Nelly wasn't about to give up. He was willing to do whatever he had to do to put St. Louis and the St. Lunatics on the map. The group began working on a new demo CD which would be taken to all the major labels in hopes of making a deal. They called it "Country Grammar," and they took a very raw version to the same DJ at Club Casino who'd played their earlier work. He liked the song so much he put it on two or three times a night.

Nelly felt like he was holding the winning lottery ticket.

In many ways he was. The song attracted attention from Cudda, who owned Reel Enter-tainment and had managed the career of Mase, a well-known hip-hop artist. Cudda got a copy of the demo and took it to At-lanta-based Universal Records. The timing was perfect. An ex-ecutive there named Kevin Law was starting a new division for hip-hop. He listened to the tape and realized Nelly could be the division's first artist.

Universal Records didn't want the St. Lunatics. They only wanted Nelly.

There was just one problem. Universal didn't want the St. Lunatics. They only wanted Nelly.

Nelly Haynes faced a tough decision. He could sign with Universal as a solo act, but that would mean leaving his old crew behind. If he stuck by the St. Lunatics, and refused to go solo, they could all fail.

Country Grammar

*T*here's an old saying in the music industry, "You leave the party with the one who brought you." That means you don't abandon the people who helped you become a success just when you're starting to be successful.

Unfortunately there is another tradition in the music industry that is just as old: separating lead singers from the rest of their band. Sometimes record label executives truly believe that the backing band isn't talented enough. Most of the time the labels just want to play it safe. They feel it's less risky to use experienced professional studio musicians to back up unknown artists.

Lead singers who go along with this often become rich and famous while the rest of their band is lucky to play weddings and hotel bars on weekends. Nelly

Successful hip-hop acts require more than just lyrical skills. They need an exciting stage show as well. Here Nelly performs at the 2003 Grammy Awards in New York City.

wanted to keep his Missouri team together, but the team wanted him to succeed. They wanted him to go solo.

"Well, it wasn't my idea, it was a group idea," Nelly told MTV. "We sat down and I want to tell everybody it's not Nelly and the St. Lunatics, it's Nelly *from* the St. Lunatics, 'cause I'm still in the group, always will be in the group, started in the group and I ain't never leavin' the group. But it was something we all decided on."

So Nelly decided to sign with Universal as a solo act. He kept his creative freedom. The label agreed to release a St. Lunatics CD if Nelly's solo album did well. The St. Lunatics would also tour with Nelly.

The crew quickly realized Universal wasn't betting big money on them. "We had three weeks in a little studio and a little bitty budget," he told *Rolling Stone.* "When you hungry, it don't matter. We'd do two songs in a day. When you from where we from, you waitin' for your shot, that's all you lookin' for."

Major labels often spend hundreds of thousands of dollars on a debut CD. Nelly made do with far less. To him it didn't matter. He finally had his chance.

"My whole purpose was to make people who speak Country Grammar not ashamed of how they talk," he explained to *Teen People,* "and turn it into the hot slang. *Country Grammar* is a celebration of having a national album come out of St. Louis. We're on a whole other level now, so let's kick it and in St. Louis *we kick it.*"

The low-budget production didn't affect the final product. Music industry magazines began reporting on Nelly and his debut CD months before it arrived. MTV began playing the *Country Grammar* video. Nelly's suave looks, smooth voice and catchy beats attracted a wide audience beyond hip-hop fans. His single was released in February 2000 and quickly rose to Number One on Billboard's

Major labels often spend hundreds of thousands of dollars on a debut CD. Nelly made do with far less.

Rap Singles chart. With a hook taken from a play-ground rhyme and Nelly's unique voice it began to be played on pop stations. "I don't sound like anyone… I'm rappin' the blues," he told *Jet Magazine*.

His audience's gender make-up was the opposite of most other hip-hop shows. It was obvious right from the beginning that far more young women were attending than young men.

"I got a lot of female fans," Nelly told *Rolling Stone*. "Well, don't get mad at me because I appeal more to women. I can't help it, I'm sorry. It would have been

Mainstream success means mainstream opportunities for Nelly. Here he appears on The Tonight Show with Jay Leno *alongside rappers P. Diddy (L) and Murphy Lee (R).*

better if I was ugly." If the rapper was ugly, he was sure he'd get more respect from people.

Still, enough people respected him to buy his music. By the end of August his album would reach Number One, and would go on to sell over eight million copies. The way he'd dealt with stress when it was the ninth inning with the bases loaded and two strikes as he waited for the perfect pitch, came into play again.

"You have a lifetime to do your first album and eighteen months for your second," Nelly explained backstage at the Billboard Music Awards in 2001. "It's just a matter of drawing on the talent I have inside." He knew the second album would prove whether or not Nelly was a one-hit wonder.

> *It was obvious from the beginning that far more young women were attending his concerts than young men.*

Nellyville

*C*ountry Grammar didn't just sell well. It earned Nelly a bucket of awards. By the end of 2001, he'd earned everything from Favorite Hip-Hop Artist at the American Music Awards to Artist of the Year at the Billboard Awards.

However, most music professionals consider the Grammy the highest honor a recording artist can achieve. Nelly was nominated for several Grammys in both 2001 and 2002. Both years he lost. It was a disappointment, but considering the drama of the last two years, it almost didn't register.

The worst was losing a member of his crew to prison. Lavell "City Spud" Webb, Nelly's half-brother, was sentenced to 10 years in jail for robbery.

"We're not sure when he's getting out," Nelly told *Rolling Stone.* 'We're working on that."

Success in the music business can mean fans, money, and awards. Nelly has enjoyed all three — here he accepts the new artist award at the first annual BET awards on June 19, 2001.

The year wasn't just about disappointments. Nelly's song "#1" was the first song on the soundtrack of the Denzel Washington film *Training Day*. Just as important, the St. Lunatics got to release their own CD. Although *Free City* wasn't nearly the best-seller *Country Grammar* was, it proved that the group could stick together no matter what the obstacles might be.

The year 2002 opened with Nelly's hometown Rams in the Super Bowl. He was invited to perform during the halftime show. It was "the highlight of my life," he confessed to *People Magazine*. Of course that highlight

Nelly tries to outdo himself at every performance. Here he prepares for an aerial routine during a rehearsal for the 45th annual Grammy Awards.

was clouded a bit by the Rams' loss to the New England Patriots in one of the closest Super Bowl games ever.

The year's focus was his follow-up CD. In its title song, "Nellyville," the rapper imaged a mythical place where everyone had 40 acres and a pool. Nelly was the mayor of Nellyville.

The question was, would audiences re-elect him?

The answer came on June 25. *Nellyville* entered the Billboard 200 album chart at Number One. Its sales were helped by the summer song "Hot in Herre," the extra "r" a nod to the "Country Grammar" pronunciation of Nelly's home state.

"I started playing with it and it just came to me," Nelly told *Billboard* magazine describing how he created the tune. "I think everyone's been to that party where it's real hot, but it was so off the chain you didn't want to leave. You'd rather start taking off clothes than leave."

While Nelly was thrilled by the audience response, he was stunned when music critics and even fellow hip-hop artists accused him of selling out and "going pop." Many even pointed to his collaborations with boy band star Justin Timberlake as proof.

"Justin is a fan of hip-hop," Nelly told the *New York Times*. "It's all hip-hop, but you got people trying to divide it saying what it is and what it's not. You going to walk into a roomful of kids and tell them they wrong?"

Nelly suffered more critical wrath when he made his movie debut. *Snipes* was a low-budget thriller. Nelly co-starred in it as an angry artist writing songs for a mobster. The movie failed to attract much notice.

Nelly was stunned when fellow hip-hop artists accused him of selling out and "going pop."

Nelly's big notice arrived with four nominations for the 2003 Grammys. This time his year had finally arrived. He picked up a pair of awards, one for Male Rap Solo Performance and another for his collaboration with

Here Nelly performs with Kelly Rowland at the 2002 Soul Train Lady of Soul Awards. Their song "Dilemma" won them a Grammy in 2003.

Kelly Rowland of Destiny's Child. His hard work had been rewarded.

The year 2003 also brought Nelly's entry into a new field: NASCAR, or the National Association for Stock Car Racing. He bought a part interest in the Craftsman Truck team. One reason was to promote his Vokal clothing line.

Nelly began Vokal with several partners in 1997. Originally they sold hats and T-shirts out of the back of a car. The company went national late in 2001 with a product line that includes velour and fleece loungewear in addition to athletic wear. In 2003, Vokal introduced its women's line, Apple Bottoms.

In addition to NASCAR fans around the country, Nelly attracted a fan in his home state. Missouri Governor Bob Holden honored Nelly and the St. Lunatics with a state proclamation for doing things such as starting a charity called 4 Sho 4 Kids. It offers medical treatment and literacy programs for disadvantaged young people in St. Louis.

"They're to be applauded for giving back to a community that has embraced them," Holden told reporter Steven Chean.

Nelly also speaks freely to kids about rising above his troubled background.

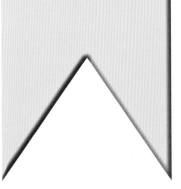

Nelly began his clothing line selling hats and T-shirts out of the back of a car in 1997.

As he told Chean, "Workin' with the 'Tics saved me when people on my block were either locked up or dead. It can be turned around, and that's what I try to tell kids living the same way I was.

"I'm a competitor. I've spent my whole life listening to people tell me I can't, I won't and I'm not. You say I can't, I will."

That means he'll continue to make music, and teach the rest of the world about St. Louis and country grammar.

CHRONOLOGY

1978   Born on November 2 in Austin, Texas to Rhoda Mack and Cornell Haynes, Sr.

1986   Rhoda and Cornell Sr. divorce

1993   Moves to University City, Missouri; Nelly and friends from University High School form the St. Lunatics

1996   St. Lunatics' song "Gimme What Ya Got" becomes a local hit; birth of daughter Chanel

1997   Begins clothing line called Vokal

1998   Signs with Universal as a solo artist

1999   Birth of son Tre

2000   Releases *Country Grammar* and is nominated for a Grammy Award

2001   Records first song on *Training Day* soundtrack

2002   Releases *Nellyville*

2003   Wins two Grammy awards

DISCOGRAPHY

1996   *Gimme What Ya Got*

2000   *Country Grammar*

2001   *Free City*

2002   *Nellyville*

SELECTED AWARDS

2001   BET Award - Best New Artist
2001   MTV Video Music Award – Best Rap Video ("Ride Wit Me")
2001   Soul Train Award – Best New Artist
2002   American Music Award – Favorite Hip-Hop Artist
2002   Billboard Music Award – Artist of the Year
2003   Soul Train Award - Sammy Davis Jr. Award for Entertainer of the Year
2003   Soul Train Award - Album of the Year (*Nellyville*)
2003   Grammy - Best Male Rap Solo Performance ("Hot in Herre")
2003   Grammy - Best Rap/Sung Collaboration (with Kelly Rowland for "Dilemma")
2003   American Music Award - Fan's Choice Award

FOR FURTHER READING

Bozza, Anthony. "Nelly." *Rolling Stone*. Nov. 9, 2000, p. 54.

Habib, Daniel G. "Q &A: Nelly." *Sports Illustrated*. Aug. 19, 2002, p. 20.

Hall, Rashaun. "Nelly's World Heated Up in 2002." *Billboard,* Dec. 7, 2002, p. 21.

People Magazine. "Nelly." Dec. 31, 2002, p. 136.

Sanneh, Kalefa. "The Mayor of Nellyville." *New York Times*, June 23, 2002, p. 21.

Sheffiled, Rob. "Shimmy-Shimmy to Nelly's Playground Chic." *Rolling Stone*, Oct. 26, 2000, p. 32.

Wasfie, Giselle. "Go Nelly." *Teen People*, Aug. 2002, p. 120.

On the Web:

MTV.com's Bands A-Z: Nelly
http://www.mtv.com/bands/az/nelly/artist.jhtml

Nelly (Universal Records)
http://www.nelly.net

A Battle for Belonging
http://www.usaweekend.com/02_issues/020519/
020519nelly.html

Good Grammar
http://www.citybeat.com/2000-12-14/music2.shtml